I0030769

Coach Cheri's Business Planning Guide for Real Estate Investors

By Cheri Alguire

& Katrina Eileen

How to set, plan and achieve all of your business and life goals using an easy step-by-step system.

Info@CheriAlguire.com

CheriAlguire.com
KatrinaEileen.com
RealEstateBusinessPlanningGuide.com
ProBusinessAndLifeCoach.com
CoachCheri.com

Copyright © 2005-2021 Cheri Alguire

Printed in the United States of America

Alguire, Cheri / Coach Cheri's Business Planning Guide for Real Estate Investors

ISBN: 9780984332366

1. Business   2. Entrepreneurship   3. Business Development

Published by Grow to Greatness Publishing
A Division of NLS Consulting, LLC
Livingston, TX

Cover Design: Brett Miller
Edited by: Cheri Alguire
Front Cover Photo: © fotopak / Adobe Stock
Back Cover Photo of Cheri Alguire: Ashton Boni
Back Cover Photo of Katrina Eileen: Mandi Ashland

CheriAlguire.com
KatrinaEileen.com
RealEstateBusinessPlanningGuide.com
ProBusinessAndLifeCoach.com
CoachCheri.com

First Edition: January 2015
Updated November 2020

For more information, email: Info@CheriAlguire.com

Coach Cheri's
BUSINESS Planning Guide

Table of Contents

A Message from Coach Cheri Alguire 1
A Message from Katrina Eileen 5

SECTION A: The Big *WHY* 7
Part 1 - What is Your Purpose? 7
Part 2 - What are Your Values? 11

SECTION B: Vision – Goal Setting 15
Part 3 – The Year in Review 15
Part 4 – Is your Life in Balance? 19
Part 5 - Is Your Business Running Smoothly? 23
Part 6 – Looking at Problem Areas 29
Part 7 – Business Review 35
Part 8 – Goal Setting 39
Part 9 – Production Goals 45

SECTION C: Creating an Action Plan to Achieve Your Goals **49**
Part 10 – Define Your Niche & Value Proposition 49
Part 11 – Lead Generation/Marketing Plan 53
Part 12 – Define Your Team Organizational Structure 57
Part 13 – Development Plan 61
Part 14 – Budgeting 65
Part 15 – Production Plan 69
Part 16 – Time and Delegation Chart 71

SECTION D: How do I get there from here? 75
Part 17 - Creating a Master Project List 75

Conclusion: 83

A Message from Coach Cheri Alguire

Congratulations on being in a rare group. Do you realize how few Real Estate Investors even bother to set goals, let alone create a plan to reach them?

For over twenty years, I have coached thousands of real estate and small business professionals to examine their values, set goals, figure out where they are right now and then created a PLAN to hit those goals.

So many Investors I meet say their goal is to do "as much as they can." When I ask them what that means in terms of Production Volume, Gross Closed Commission, Net Commission or Profit, I am met with blank stares.

And when I ask them to dream ahead of how they want their life to be in five years, many Investors look downright distressed. I'm asked, "How could I possibly look so far into an unknown future? Who could make a plan not knowing what is going to happen?"

Well, whether you realize it or not, the next five years will be a blur…. and when you get there you will either be asking yourself where the time went and bemoaning that you just didn't have the time to accomplish anything or…

You can smile into the mirror with the realization that you took the time to plan out where you wanted to be and, not only arrived there, but far surpassed even your most outrageous and what seemed unreachable goals.

It can be done!

The power of planning is incredible. It all starts with a far-out unattainable dream. Then simply add in the baby steps it will take along the way and you're almost there.

I've designed this 17 part-planning workbook in response to the needs of many Real Estate Agents who have been awed by what they perceive as a near impossible task. It isn't!

To get where <u>you</u> want to be, you need to ask yourself these basic questions:

- Where am I now?
- Where do I see myself in five years?
- How do I bridge that gap?

The questions and charts in this workbook will walk you step by step through this important and life-changing process.

How to Get The Most Out of this Business Planning Guide
The workbook you are about to go through will walk you through the same exact process I have coached new and experienced agents through with astounding results. Whether you have a team, are a solo agent, are a new agent or have been around for years, this workbook is perfect for you!

I want to warn you not to "skip" any of the sections. I know you may want to go right into the Production Goals, Marketing Plan or even Budgeting sections, however, I am asking you to trust the process. It works.

By focusing on your "Why", your purpose and values first it will help you set goals that are just the right size, not too small, nor too big that fit with your life goals. By focusing on where you are right now and what is currently working, we will be able to create the best possible plans for Production, Lead Generation and your Delegation Chart.

Free Business Planning Workbook Review Session:
As a reward for finishing what you start, I will give you a free one-on-one coaching call with me (a $297 value) once you finish this workbook. All you need to do is contact me through my website at CheriAlguire.com and mention you would like to schedule your free Business Planning Workbook Review Session.

The time to design your future is now!
Be bold and get ready to take your business and life to the next level. And just like everything we do, let's get going, one step at a time…

Coach Cheri Alguire
info@CheriAlguire.com
949-916-3289

A Message from Katrina Eileen

Which comes first? The mindset or the success? I would argue that you should focus on both at the same time.

Mindset will allow you to bring into focus where you are going, and then allow you to see new opportunities. *Success* will give you the needed experience that causes you to change your mindset.

So where does a Real Estate Entrepreneur begin?

No matter where you are at right now or what level you are investing at, the most powerful action you can take is to create a plan... complete this Business Planning Guide!

As you go through this guide, your vision of where you are going and why you are going there will create a path that will open up in front of you. What's next becomes simple... you will see opportunities where you didn't before.

I have met so many investors and brokers who have invested thousands of dollars and hundreds of hours into their education and training in this area. I have met only a few who have answered these questions:

Why should a seller sell to me?

How do I increase my profit and create value for everyone involved?

How many flips, wholesale deals, and long term hold properties do I need to achieve my goals?

How many dollars will I need to borrow or lend this year to create the income to take me to the next level?

With a clear purpose and specific actions to take, the "what's next" becomes very simple and will keep you operating in line with your values and beliefs. The process this Guide takes you through can bring balance, fullness and meaning to your life and your entrepreneurial endeavors.

Game On!

Katrina Eileen
Real Estate Investor

SECTION A: The Big *WHY*
Part 1 - What is Your Purpose?

Purpose provides the foundation of our values, vision and goals. Purpose gives meaning to everything we do in our personal and professional lives, yet not all of us recognize our purpose or can articulate it. The following questions will help you uncover your purpose.

LIFE:

▶ What are the things that give you the most joy in your life?

▶ When do you feel the most satisfied?

▶ What is truly important to you?

▶ What are you most proud of having accomplished at this point in your life?

▶ What do you want for yourself and others in your personal life?

▶ What do you want to leave for others after you are gone? What do you want your legacy to be? What would you want people to say about you at your funeral?

▶ A "Purpose Statement" for your life is a few sentences that summarize your "WHY" for life. What really matters for YOU? What are YOU all about? What is your "Life Purpose Statement"?

BUSINESS:

► Have you had a time, professionally, in the past year when you have said, "This is why I do what I do every day"? Describe that experience.

► Why are you a Real Estate Investor?

► What do you want, professionally, for your sellers and buyers?

► What do you offer that is unique and/or excites you?

► If you were financially able to retire one year from today, what would you want to do in your Real Estate Investment Business that you haven't done yet?

► A "Purpose Statement" for your business is a few sentences that describe the "WHY" you have a business in real estate investment. What is your purpose statement for your business?

Business and Life Purpose Statements can provide a basis for creating a vision and goals that are truly meaningful. They can also help drive us daily to do the things we need to do to reach our goals.

PART 2 - What are Your Values?

Your values are at the core of your personality and influence the way you respond to people and events. Your core values dictate what is important in both life and business: how business should be conducted, your view of humanity, and your role in society. Your core values are always at work in the background and are always present as a shaping force. They come from inside you and are an authentic extension of what you hold in your gut. Values direct and motivate us towards certain goals.

► **Below is a list of different values.** Circle the 5 values you would consider most important in your life:

• Adventure	• Financial	• Peace
• Affection	• Responsibility	• Perseverance
• Authenticity	• Freedom	• Playfulness
• Balance	• Friendship	• Power
• Beauty	• Generosity	• Privacy
• Challenge	• Grace	• Punctuality
• Clarity	• Growth	• Relationships
• Commitment	• Happiness	• Respect
• Community	• Harmony	• Responsibility
• Compassion	• Health	• Security
• Confidence	• Honesty	• Sincerity
• Connection	• Humor	• Solitude
• Contribution	• Integrity	• Spirituality
• Courage	• Joy	• Success
• Creativity	• Kindness	• Trust
• Diversity	• Knowledge	• Truthfulness
• Duty	• Leadership	• Wealth
• Energetic	• Love	• Wisdom
• Equality	• Loyalty	• Other
• Excellence	• Mastery	
• Faith	• Passion	
• Family	• Patience	

➤ Name 3 people you most admire. What values do they hold? Why do you admire them?

-

-

-

For each of the top five values you circled, complete this sentence:

- Was I in alignment with my value of _____ in my business and my life this past year? How? How am I going to continue or improve on that for next year?

- Was I in alignment with my value of _____ in my business and my life this past year? How? How am I going to continue or improve on that for next year?

- Was I in alignment with my value of _____ in my business and my life this past year? How? How am I going to continue or improve on that for next year?

- Was I in alignment with my value of _____ in my business and my life this past year? How? How am I going to continue or improve on that for next year?

- Was I in alignment with my value of _____ in my business and my life this past year? How? How am I going to continue or improve on that for next year?

The first step in planning goals is figuring out who you are, what is in your gut, so you can come up with goals that are in alignment with your core values. Next, we will explore the process of creating the vision.

SECTION B: Vision – Goal Setting
Part 3 – The Year in Review

Sometimes life seems to get so busy and you are constantly working on the list of to-dos that you don't take the time to stop and evaluate your life. It is important to recognize everything you have done this year, celebrate the accomplishments and also look at what may have stopped you short of reaching a goal. This process will help you to learn from your successes and shortcomings and apply these lessons to achieving your long-term goals.

▶ What did you accomplish this year?

▶ What is the greatest thing that has happened to you in the past year?

▶ What are some things that happened in the past year that you want to duplicate?

▶ What was challenging in this past year?

▶ What do you not want to have happen again?

▶ What did you learn from going through these experiences of the past year?

▶ What has prevented you from achieving your goals in the past?

▶ What were some of the most important decisions of the past year for you?

▶ What decision might you make next year as a result of those decisions?

▶ What was something in your life that was once just a goal or dream, which at the time seemed extremely difficult or impossible to achieve, but has since become reality?

▶ How did you make that goal a reality? What steps did you go through? Did you create and follow a plan to achieve it? What are you going to take from this experience to use when creating a plan for this year's goals?

Next, we will complete our life balance diagnostic.

Part 4 – Is your Life in Balance?

▶ Sometimes we focus our energies so much on a few areas of our life that we forget that other areas are also important. Which areas have you neglected recently? The *Wheel of Life*, sometimes called the *Balance Wheel*, will help you visualize your current situation. It will provide a snapshot of how you see your life today. Each spoke in the Balance Wheel represents an area in your life that can contribute to your feeling of happiness and satisfaction.

▶ Now, you will NEVER be in total balance, however, it is important to acknowledge the areas of your life you may have been neglecting in pursuit of your other goals. If you wish, you can make the wheel more meaningful by changing any of the eight aspects given here. Give yourself a score based on your current level of satisfaction with each. This does not mean you are to grade yourself compared to other's success based on society's ideals. This is about *you* and how you feel right now about your life. Rank the eight areas in the Wheel of Life on a scale of 1-10 (1 being completely dissatisfied and 10 being completely fulfilled)

1. **Career/Business/Work** _____ **(1-10)**

2. **Social /Friendships** _____ **(1-10)**

3. **Community/Service/Charity** _____ **(1-10)**

4. **Financial/Money/Lifestyle** _____ **(1-10)**

5. **Physical/Fitness/Health** _____ **(1-10)**

6. **Spiritual Growth** _____ **(1-10)**

7. **Family/Love/Relationships** _____ **(1-10)**

8. **Mental/Personal Growth** _____ **(1-10)**

Fill in the segments on this graph with your scores to get a visual representation of how your life is balanced.

Life Balance Wheel

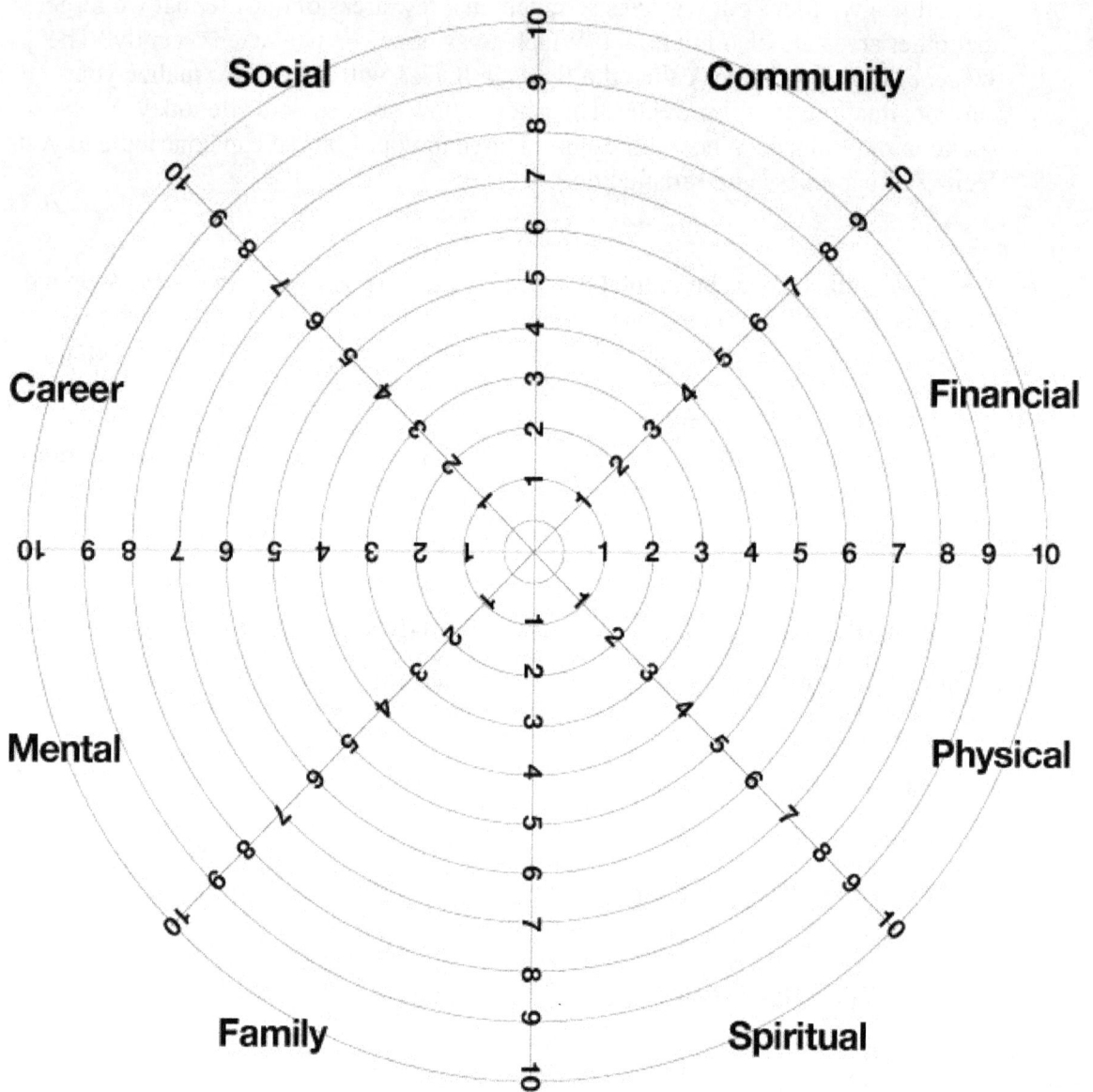

Now connect the dots. How would your car travel if the wheels were in this shape? If half of the wheel is flat or if it is an odd shape and not round you will have problems gaining momentum in all areas of your life.

▶ What would you need to do in each of the 8 areas to raise the number to a 10 within the next year? Place a star next to the 2-3 areas that you would most like to improve.

1. Career

2. Social

3. Community

4. Financial

5. Physical

6. Spiritual

7. Family

8. Mental

This exercise should be repeated at least quarterly to once again get this mental snapshot of which areas you may be neglecting and why you may be having trouble gaining momentum.

In this section, we looked at your life overall. Next, we will begin to review what happened in your business this past year.

Part 5 - Is Your Business Running Smoothly?

Now let's take that same overall process and break it down to your business. Just like in the previous exercise where we looked at your life overall, let's take some time to break down that first section call Career/Business/Work into 8 segments so we can analyze how smoothly your business is running currently. The sections include:

Marketing and Lead Generation Systems: All Online and Offline Marketing that will help you find these three things; Buyers and Sellers, Product and Capital, Including, but are not limited to: Website, Social Media, Internet Leads, Networking Events, Relationship Marketing, Direct Mail, Expired Leads, FSBOs, Video Marketing, and any type of advertising including interactions with you Database and/or Sphere of Influence

Capital Sources: Your working capital for investment; Cash on Hand, Private Money Lenders, Hard Money Lenders, Self-Directed IRA's, Sellers, Individual Investors, Joint Venture Partners

People Systems: Assistants, Listing Broker and other team members, (Outside Salesperson, Project Managers, etc.) and preferred Vendors (Loan Officers, Title Representatives, Escrow Partner, Plumbers, Electricians, Handymen, General Contractors, Painters, Landscapers, Designers, Lighting Consultants)

Costing & Project Management Model: a "duplicate-able" and "scale-able" model for your modes of investing (i.e. budgets, scopes of work, timelines and contractual agreements for each type of Investment Property you plan on engaging with, Joint Venture, or Investment Dollars you will have out on loan)

Technology Systems: Database Management, Transaction Coordination, Email Marketing, Blogging System, Smart Phones, Tablets, Computers, and Communication Systems.

Support Systems: Systems in place to support your big picture planning, goal setting & attainment of goals; Accountant, Financial Planner, Legal, Family, and Coaching

Income from All Sources: Flips, Margin, Assignments, Interest Income, Joint Ventures

Bottom Line Profit: Your net profit as a percentage of all Gross Income

When your business is running smoothly, these eight areas are all in sync. If you wish, you can make the wheel more meaningful by changing any of the eight aspects given here. Give yourself a score based on your current level of satisfaction with each on a scale of 1-10 (1 being completely dissatisfied and 10 being completely satisfied)

1. **Marketing/Lead Generation Systems** _____ **(1-10)**

2. **Capital Sources** _____ **(1-10)**

3. **People Systems** _____ **(1-10)**

4. **Costing & Project Management Model** _____ **(1-10)**

5. **Technology Systems** _____ **(1-10)**

6. **Support Systems of Big Picture** _____ **(1-10)**

7. **Income from All Sources** _____ **(1-10)**

8. **Bottom Line Profit** _____ **(1-10)**

Business Wheel

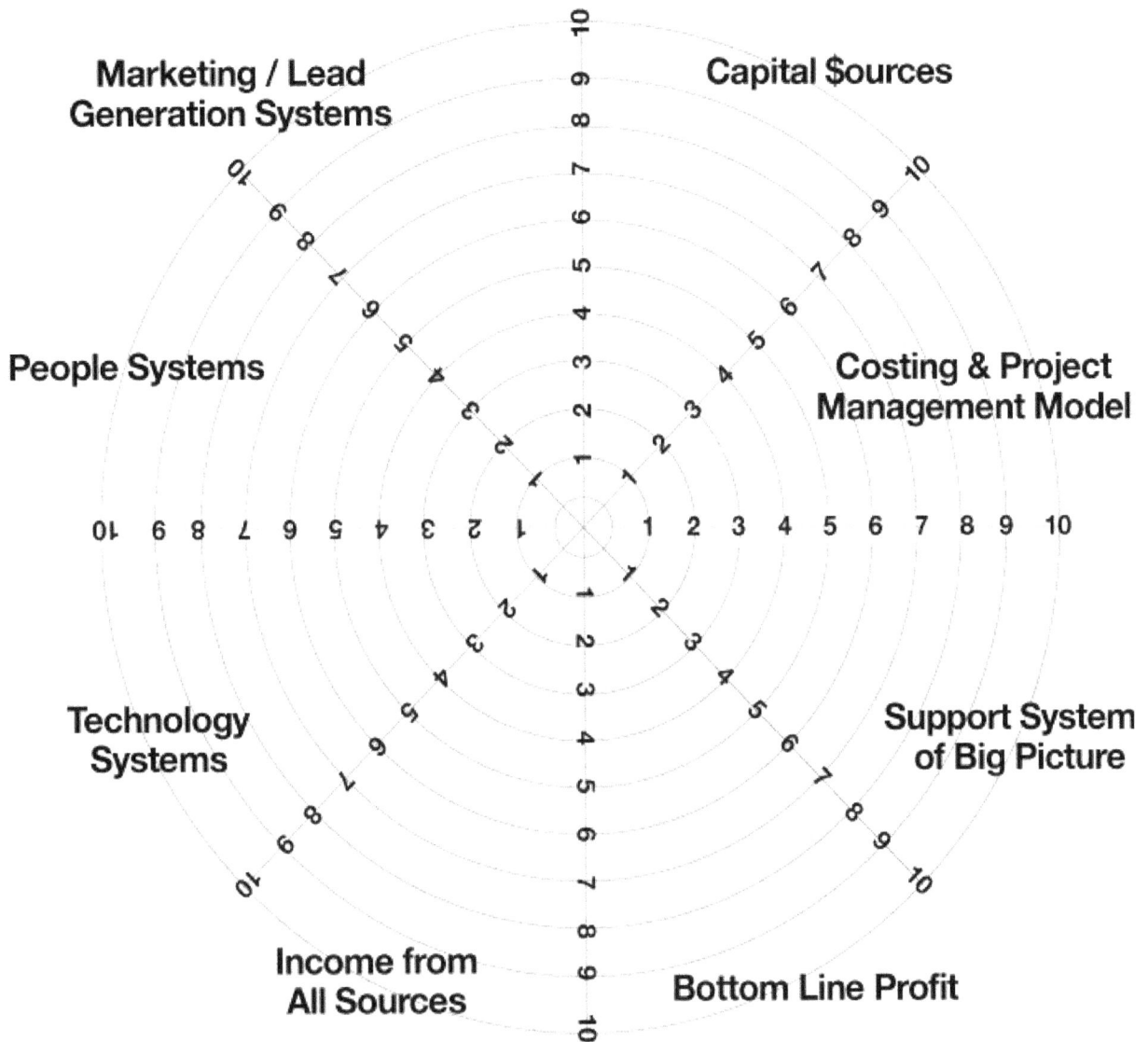

Now connect the dots. How would your car travel if the wheels were in this shape? If half of the wheel is flat or if it is an odd shape and not round you will have problems gaining momentum.

What would you need to do in each of the 8 areas to raise the number to a 10 within the next year? Place a star next to the 2-3 areas that you would most like to improve.

1. Marketing and Lead Generation

2. Capital Sources

3. People Systems

4. Costing & Project Management Model

5. Technology Systems

6. Support Systems for Big Picture Planning/Goal Setting

7. Income from All Sources

8. Bottom Line Profit (Net)

This exercise should be repeated at least quarterly to once again get this mental snapshot of which areas you may be neglecting and why you may be having trouble gaining momentum.

Part 6 – Looking at Problem Areas

This eight segment process can be used to dissect any area of the Balance Wheel that is either extremely low or is an area that you repeatedly have problems with

Below you will see an example of how to break down the Physical/Health section of the Life Balance Wheel. You could also use the blank wheel to break down a particular problem area of the Business Wheel. There are blank lines to the right of the numbers if you want to break down another section of the Life Wheel.

Give yourself a score based on your current level of satisfaction with each area of this Custom Wheel on a scale of 1-10 (1 being completely dissatisfied and 10 being completely satisfied)

1. **Exercise** _____ (1-10) _____

2. **Diet/Foods** _____ (1-10) _____

3. **Weight Management** _____ (1-10) _____

4. **Hydration/Water** _____ (1-10) _____

5. **Unhealthily Habits** _____ (1-10) _____

6. **Stress Management** _____ (1-10) _____

7. **Sleep** _____ (1-10) _____

8. **Vitamins/Supplements** _____ (1-10) _____

Again, fill in the segments below with your scores to get a visual representation of how your custom area is balanced.

Health Wheel

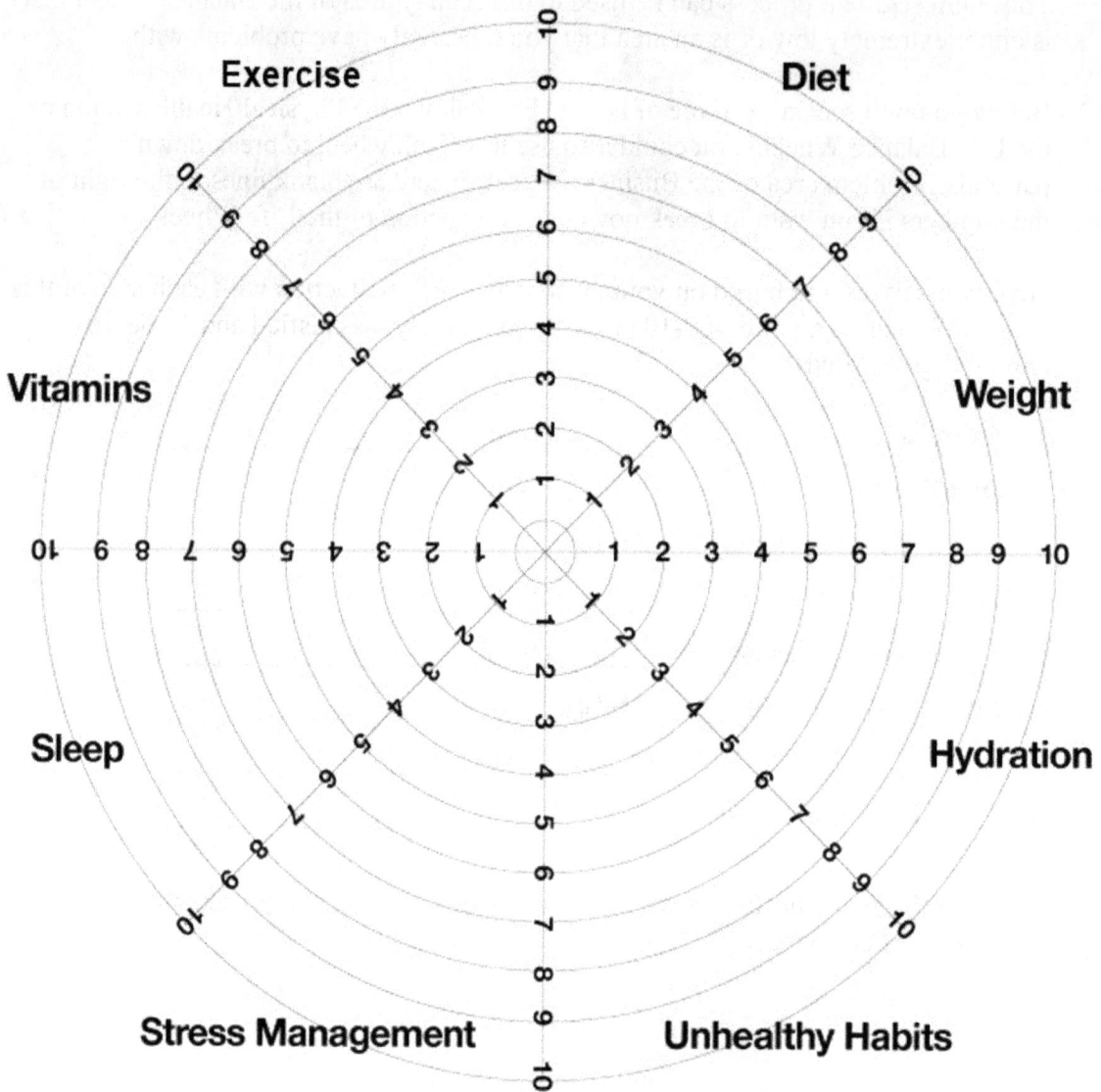

Now connect the dots. How would your car travel if the wheels were in this shape? If half of the wheel is flat or if it is an odd shape and not round you will have problems gaining momentum in all areas of your life

Custom Wheel

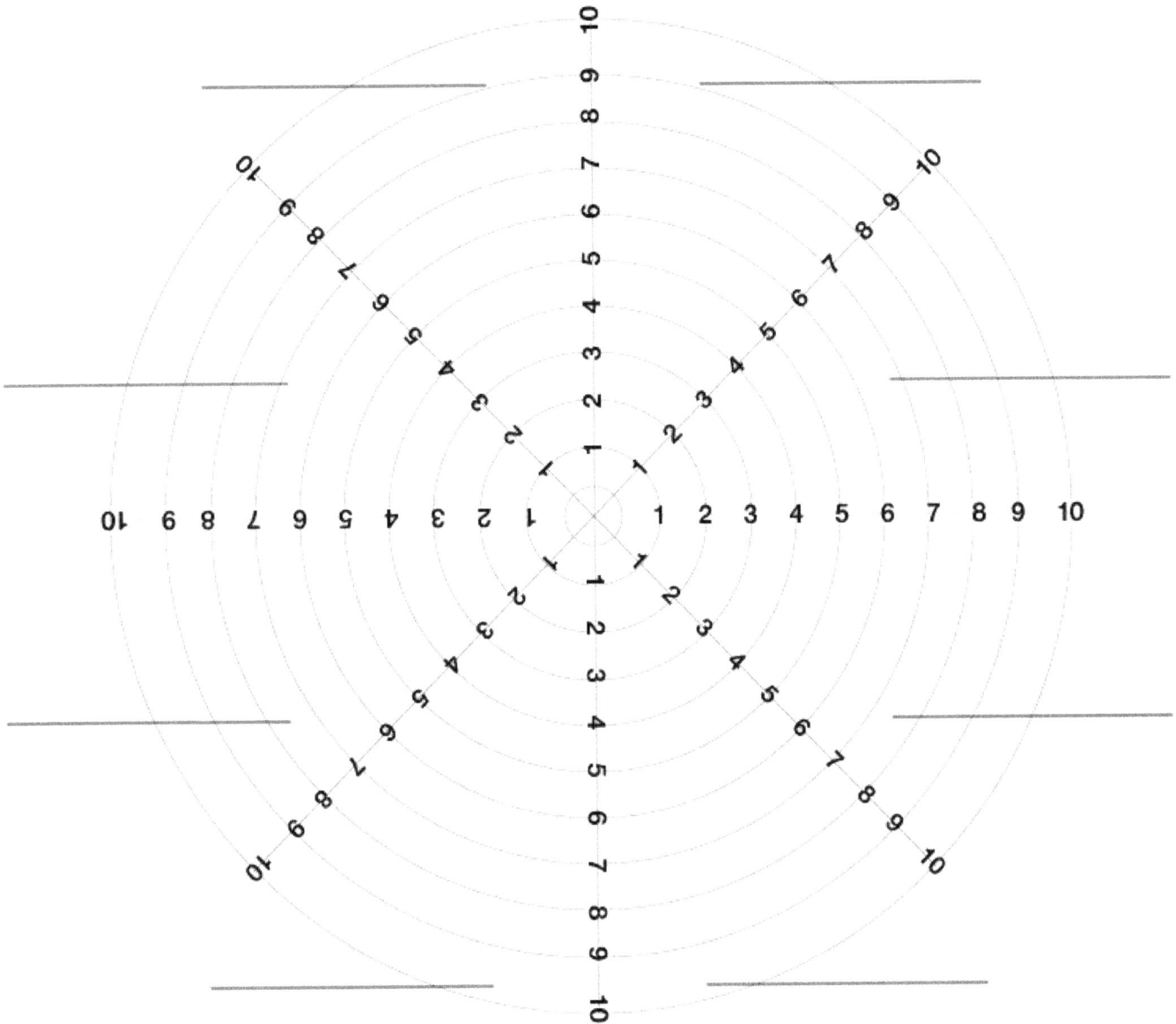

Now connect the dots. How would your car travel if the wheels were in this shape? If half of the wheel is flat or if it is an odd shape and not round you will have problems gaining momentum in all areas of your life.

What would you need to do in each of the 8 areas of your Health/Custom area to raise the number to a 10 within the next year? Place a star next to the 2-3 areas that you would most like to improve.

1. _____

2. _____

3. _____

4. _____

5. _____

6. _____

7. _____

8. _____

This exercise should be repeated at least quarterly to once again get this mental snapshot of which areas you may be neglecting and why you may be having trouble gaining momentum.

	Goal	Year-End	+ / -
Gross Revenue			
Gross Revenue Assignments			
Gross Revenue Flips			
Gross Margin Income			
Gross Revenue from Capital on Loan			
Net Revenue			
Expenses			
Expense % of Net Revenue			
# of Transactions			
# of Assignments			
# of Flips			
# of Lease Options and/or Wrap Notes			
Amount of Capital Out on Loan / Interest Rate			
Interest Dollars Earned			

Part 7 – Business Review

Take a review of your business for the last 12 months. (May have to estimate)

	Goal	Year-End	+ / -
Acquisition & Buyer Lead Sources:			
# of Acquisitions Taken (*from above*)			
Database (Past Sellers with More Properties, Buyers Sellers, Sphere…)			
Referral Business (From Past Acquisitions, Investment Groups…)			
Online (Website, Social Media…)			
Online Paid Ads (Zillow, Google or Facebook…)			
FSBO/Expireds/Bank Owned			
Direct Mail/ Door Knocking			
Other (List other sources*)			
Capital Lead Sources:			
Database (Private Investment Dollars)			
Investment groups, REIA's			
Hard Money Lenders			
Sellers			
J. V. Partners			
Other (List other sources*)			

► Did you hit your goals?

► What did you do to achieve these results?

► Describe your team: Who do you have and what are their roles?

► Describe your lead generation this year:

► What were the best sources of your leads in the past 12 months?

► Summarize what happened in your business this year.

► How many hours a week did you work on average?

► How much vacation time did you take this year?

Now that you have finished looking at where you are at the end of the past 12 months, you will begin goal setting for next year with part 8.

Part 8 – Goal Setting

▶ Write down every goal you hope to accomplish in the next year. Don't hold back, dream LARGE, think BIG, aim HIGH.

■ Personal Development Goals

- Social/Friendships

- Community/Service/Charity

- Financial/Money/Lifestyle

- Spiritual

- Family/Love/Relationships

- Mental//Personal Growth

- Health

- Other

- **Business Development Goals**

  - Marketing/Lead Generation

  - Capital Sources

  - People Systems

  - Costing & Project Management Model

  - Technology Systems

  - Support Systems for Big Picture Planning/Goal Setting

  - Income from All Sources

  - Bottom Line Profit (Net)

- **Other Development Goals**

▶ When you have finished, go back and * the top 20% of your goals

▶ From your list of * goals. Rewrite the goal below in the present tense as if you have already achieved it. Then write how you will feel when this goal is a reality.

1.

2.

3.

4.

5.

Analyze your goals

▶ Do your top 5 goals meet the following "Goal Test?"

■ Are they **SMART** Goals?

- **S**pecific

- **M**easurable

- **A**greed (accountable to someone)

- **R**ealistic

- **T**imely (time-phased)

■ They also need to be **PURE** Goals

- **P**ositively stated

- **U**nderstandable

- **R**elevant

- **E**xciting

■ And **CLEAR** Goals

- **C**alculated

- **L**arge

- **E**ngaging

- **A**ppropriate

- **R**ecorded

If your goals do not quite fit the analyzing acronyms above, reword them here:

Next, we will be looking specifically at your production goals in your business. We will work the numbers to find out how many clients you need to work with to reach not only your business goals but the personal goals listed here as well.

Part 9 – Production Goals

Now it is time to work the numbers. To hit the personal and general business goals, how does that break down into specific number goals for the next one to five years? You don't have to work past next year, but I have given you the option to do so if you wish to project out 5 years.

Production Goals

	Next Year's Goal	2-year goal	3-year goal	4-year goal	5-year goal
Gross Revenue					
Gross Revenue Assignments					
Gross Revenue Flips					
Gross Margin Income					
Gross Revenue from Capital Lent					
Net Revenue					
Expenses					
Expense % of Net Revenue					
# of Transactions					
# of Assignments					
# of Flips					
# of Lease Options and/or wrap notes					
Amount of Capital Out on Loan / Interest Rate					
Interest Dollars Earned					

Acquisition Source:	Next Year's Goal	2 year goal	3 year goal	4 year goal	5 year goal
# of Listings Taken (*from above*)					
Database (Property Owners with Multiple Properties, Sphere…)					
Referral Business (From acquired Investment Groups…)					
Online (Website, Social Media…)					
Online Paid Ads (Zillow, Google or Facebook…)					
FSBO/Expireds/Bank Owned					
Direct Mail					
Other (List other sources*) Door Knocking					
Capital Lead Source:					
# Buyer Sales (*from above*)					
Database (Private Investment Dollars)					
Investment groups, REIA's					
Hard Money Lenders					
Sellers					
J. V. Partners					
Other (List Sources*)					

Now that you have specific production goals set for the next 1-5 years you will begin creating the business and marketing plan to hit those goals. Next, we will be taking a closer look at your target market and how you are going to attract business from that niche.

SECTION C: Creating an Action Plan to Achieve Your Goals
Part 10 – Define Your Niche & Value Proposition

Niche

Sometimes you choose your niche and it works out from the beginning. Other times, your niche evolves as you and your business change and grow. Remember, mass appeal equals no appeal. You can't be everything to everyone. Specialization gives people a reason to choose you. Specialization builds perceived value and being a specialist is also easier because you know your clients you can create systems so you can be more effective.

▶ Describe in detail your current niche:

▶ "Who" do you best relate to? And why?

▶ Who is your "ideal seller"?

▶ Do you need to make changes to your target market? If yes, why?

▶ Describe your target market for next year:

▶ Do you need to make any changes to your Lead Sources from Part 9?

Value Proposition

The money you make is in direct proportion to the value you provide to the marketplace. When you are clear on your value proposition, your confidence will come across to every client and prospect you communicate with.

▶ Why should a seller choose you as their buyer?

▶ What is your value proposition to buyers?

▶ What is your value proposition to sellers?

▶ Why do you deserve the profit that you will make in the acquisition?

▶ Why do you deserve the income you make in your business?

Next, we will begin looking at how you will attract your niche to you with your lead generation plan.

Part 11 – Lead Generation/Marketing Plan

To attract your niche clients to you, you must have an effective lead generation system and marketing plan in place. In Parts 9 we looked at where you anticipated the leads for the sales you are projecting will come from. You need to create a marketing plan that will work in generating the leads from the sources you are projecting. It is important to recognize what specific changes to your current plans are necessary to make in order to reach your goals.

▶ Describe your current Marketing Plan: (Marketing Plan for past year) Marketing Components and Schedule

▶ Describe your current lead generation system: This is the outbound letter, phone call, inside sales that actualizes the marketing plan.

▶ Complete the Marketing Plan Chart. Each column represents a week out of the month. You can either just use checkmarks, or you can create a code system and put letters or numbers in the boxes.

▶ What changes are you going to have to make for next year to reach your goals? Be specific.

Next, we discuss the elements that go into defining your team organizational structure.

Marketing and Lead Generation Plan

		January			February			March			April			May			June		
Relationship Marketing	Thank You																		
	Birthday																		
	Holiday																		
	Keep in touch																		
	Email Newsletter																		
	Other																		
Online Marketing	Blog post to website																		
	Paid Adverting (FB…)																		
	Social Media																		
	Zillow for their properties																		
	Other																		
Offline	Direct Mail																		
	Door Knocking																		
Networking	REIA's																		
	MeetUps																		

		July			August			September			October			November			December		
Relationship Marketing	Thank You																		
	Birthday																		
	Holiday																		
	Keep in touch																		
	Email Newsletter																		
	Other																		
Online Marketing	Blog post to website																		
	Paid Adverting (FB…)																		
	Social Media																		
	Zillow for their properties																		
	Other																		
Offline	Direct Mail																		
	Door Knocking																		
Networking	REIA's																		
	MeetUps																		

Part 12 – Define Your Team Organizational Structure

It is important to understand the Organizational Structure of your team. This includes team job descriptions and anticipated changes in the next few years. Feel free to change or add boxes to fit your team. Write people's names in the boxes. Some people may be in more than one box, even if that name is yours!

Team Organizational Chart

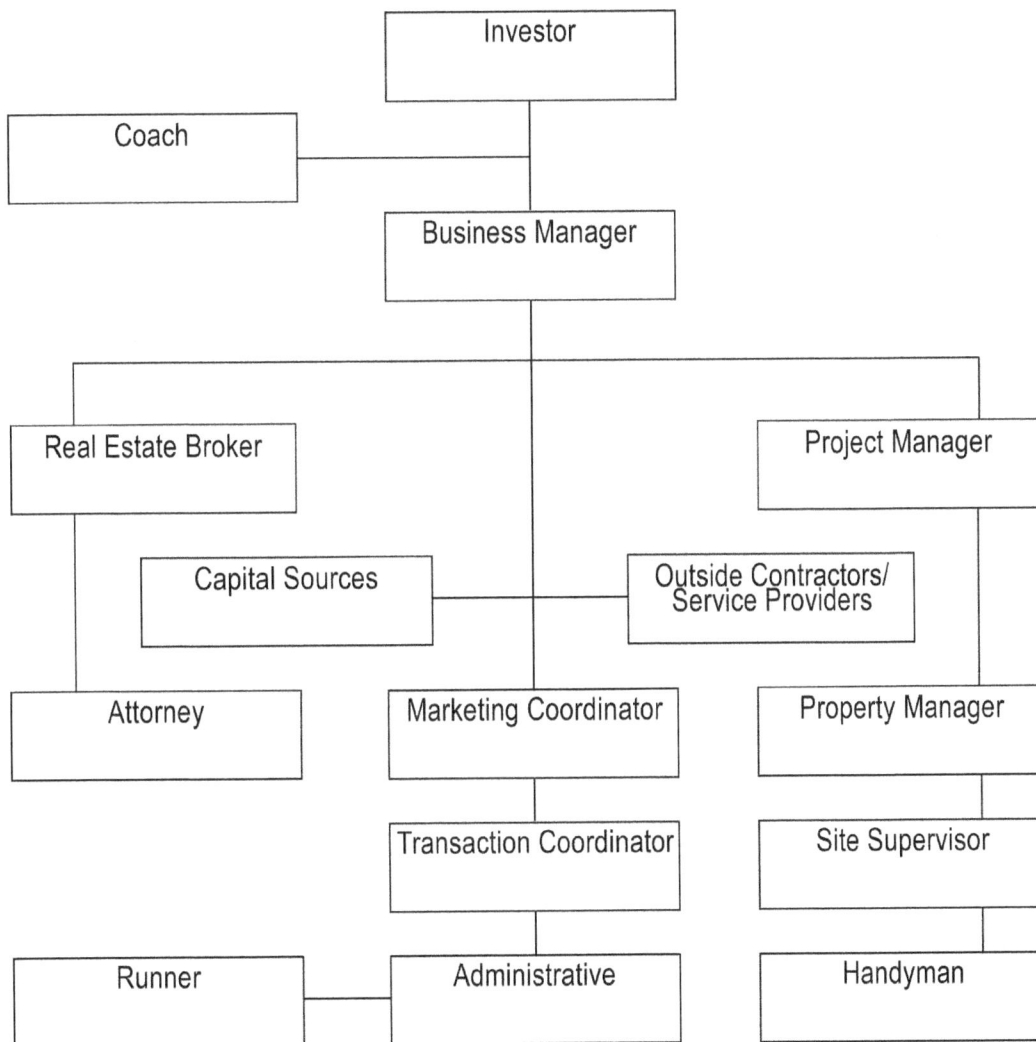

```
                        ┌─────────────────┐
                        │    Investor     │
                        └────────┬────────┘
┌─────────────────┐              │
│     Coach       │──────┬───────┘
└─────────────────┘      │
                ┌────────┴────────┐
                │ Business Manager │
                └────────┬────────┘
          ┌──────────────┴──────────────────────┐
┌─────────────────┐                    ┌─────────────────┐
│Real Estate Broker│                   │ Project Manager │
└────────┬────────┘                    └────────┬────────┘
         │   ┌─────────────────┐  ┌───────────────────────┐
         │   │ Capital Sources │──│ Outside Contractors/  │
         │   └─────────────────┘  │  Service Providers    │
         │                        └───────────────────────┘
┌─────────────────┐  ┌──────────────────────┐  ┌─────────────────┐
│    Attorney     │  │Marketing Coordinator │  │ Property Manager│
└─────────────────┘  └──────────┬───────────┘  └────────┬────────┘
                     ┌──────────────────────┐  ┌─────────────────┐
                     │Transaction Coordinator│ │ Site Supervisor │
                     └──────────┬───────────┘  └────────┬────────┘
┌─────────────────┐  ┌──────────────────────┐  ┌─────────────────┐
│     Runner      │──│    Administrative    │  │    Handyman     │
└─────────────────┘  └──────────────────────┘  └─────────────────┘
```

▶ Who is on your team?

▶ Summarize or attach their job descriptions.

▶ Describe the compensation plans with those positions.

▶ What changes do you expect to make in the next year?

▶ What changes do you expect to make in the next three years?

▶ What changes do you expect to make in the next five years?

Next, we will discuss creating a development plan, and what changes are necessary for you to make in order to reach your goals.

Part 13 – Development Plan

In order to reach your goals next year, what changes do you need to make in specific areas of your business? A *Development Plan* will list the projects you will be working on throughout the year. This is the place to capture all of those things you have wanted to research, create, do, perfect, delegate and implement in your business. You may not have something for every area.

- Marketing and Lead Generation Systems (What kinds of systems do you need to bring in the leads, lead capture, database, social media, video, special reports, lead magnets, Referral of a Lifetime Plan, Relationship Marketing Plan)

- Sales and Servicing Systems (What kinds of systems do you need to convert and keep the leads, CRM, Auto responder, CardsForRealEstate.com)

- Equipment (i.e. Computers, Camera, Drone, Tablets, Smart Phones)

- Technology (i.e. Computer Programs, Websites, Internet Marketing, Social Media, HootSuite, Apps, SEO)

- People and Staffing (i.e. Assistant, Project Manager, Outside Sales Transaction Coordinator, Marketing Manager)

- Support Systems (Coaching, Legal, Mentor, Social Media Management)

■ Training - Self (i.e. Real Estate Investment Training Seminar, Personal Growth Seminar, Script Writing, Social Media Training, Internet Marketing, Investment Coaching, Negotiation Training, Project Management Training)

■ Training - Staff (i.e. Project Management, Software Training, Team Retreat, Sales Training, Script Writing)

■ Policies (i.e. Bonus Structures, Vacation Coverage, Policies for Sales & Marketing Team or Administrative Staff, Sales and Marketing)

■ Procedures (i.e. Initial Lead Contact Procedure, File Coordination, Consistent Incoming Phone Answering Procedure, Documentation of Procedures)

■ Team Development (i.e. Adding positions, moving people within your team, increasing or setting minimum standards)

■ Other (Anything else that you have wanted to do in your business, but have not implemented yet.)

Next, we will discuss budgeting and creating an Expenses Worksheet for next year.

Part 14 – Budgeting

Below you will find a worksheet to budget your expenses for the next year. You will want to review your expenses for the current year and include any new marketing and development changes from the previous section. Most budgeting and account software, such as QuickBooks, will provide reports for you to analyze your current business expenses and will assist you in creating a budget. If you do not have that type of system in place yet, you can use these charts to help you get started.

Total Income and Expenses

	Last year Totals	Adjustment	Next Year Totals
GROSS REVENUES			
Assignments			
Flips			
Margin Income			
Interest Income			
Direct Expenses			
Outside Sales			
Referral Fees			
Bonuses			
Total Direct Expenses			
MARKETING			
Website			
SEO (Google Adwords)			
Social Media Ads			
Social Media Management			
Database			
Internet Marketing			
Incoming Lead Subscriptions			
Direct Mail			
Printed Materials: Flyers, Brochures, Business Cards			
CardsForRealEstate.com			
Gifts/Entertainment			
Radio			
Newspaper Ads			
Magazine Ads			
Billboards			
Signs			
Other			
Total Marketing Expenses			

	Last year Totals	Adjustment	Next Year Totals
OPERATING			
Salaries			
Auto Expense			
Office Rent			
Office Expenses			
Phone			
Supplies			
Equipment			
Technology			
Continuing Ed			
Association Dues			
Coaching			
Taxes			
Travel			
Transaction Coordination			
Outside Services			
Total Operating Expenses			
TOTAL OPERATING & MARKETING EXPENSES			
O & M % of NCC			
TOTAL EXPENSES			
TOTAL EXPENSE % OF NCC			
TOTAL PROFIT (NCC – Total Expenses)			
PROFIT %			

If you are not happy with these numbers, you may need to rework your development plan, marketing plan or production goals from previous sections. After you have total expenses, use the chart below to break them down to monthly expenses. This will be the chart you will use to monitor your expenses throughout the year.

Marketing and Operating Expense Monthly Budget

	JAN	FEB	MAR	APR	MAY	JUN	JUL	AUG	SEP	OCT	NOV	DEC	TOTAL
MARKETING													
Website													
SEO													
Social Media Ads													
Social Media Management													
Database													
Internet Marketing													
Lead Subscriptions													
Direct Mail													
Printed Materials													
CardsForRealEstate.com													
Gifts/Entertainment													
Radio													
Newspaper Ads													
Magazine Ads													
Billboards													
Signs													
Total Marketing Expenses													
OPERATING													
Salaries													
Auto Expense													
Office Rent													
Office Expenses													
Phone													
Supplies													
Equipment													
Technology													
Continuing Ed													
Dues													
Coaching													
Taxes													
Travel													
Transaction Coordination													
Outside Services													
Total Operating Expenses													
TOTAL													

Part 15 – Production Plan

To hit your business goals, you will need to break down a few of the key numbers from Part 9 down to quarterly and monthly goals. Take these four numbers from Part 9 and place them on the bottom of the chart under "TOTAL": Number of Closed Transactions, Number of Flips, Number of Assignments, Number of Lease Options/Wrap Notes and Amount of Capital out on Loan for next year. Work your way up the chart by breaking those numbers down by quarters based on your past trends. Then continue to break those quarterly goals down to monthly goals. These Monthly Goals are what you will have to do and monitor monthly to hit your production goals next year.

Monthly Production Plan

	TRANSACTIONS	FLIP	ASSIGNMENTS	LEASE OPTIONS	Capital on Loan Interest Income
Q-1					
JAN					
FEB					
MAR					
Q1 total					
Q-2					
APR					
MAY					
JUN					
Q2 total					
Q-3					
JUL					
AUG					
SEPT					
Q3 total					
Q-4					
OCT					
NOV					
DEC					
Q4 total					
TOTAL					

Part 16 – Time and Delegation Chart

If you are going to reach the goals you have set for this year, you are going to have to make sure you manage your time properly and delegate effectively. How are you spending your time---"IN" or "ON" your business? How do you think/feel you are spending your time? Be honest with yourself.

What percentage of your time do you spend in each of the following areas?

_____% TECHNICIAN – *entering data, filling out forms, working on files, accounting, scheduling appointments*

_____% DOER – *showing, holding opens, selling, listing, negotiating*

_____% MANAGER – *motivating, mentoring, training, tracking accountability*

_____% VISIONARY – *studying, attending speakers/seminars, developing strategic plans/steps that build/promote business*

= 100% – *of your working efforts*

It is important to remember that NO business can survive without *Technicians* attending to details and *Doers* closing deals. However, it is equally important to recognize that for a business to flourish; it must be fueled by *Vision* and guided by enlightened *Managers*.

How grounded in Vision and guided by Managing is YOUR BUSINESS?

Over the last months, on a day to day or week to week basis, what have you done that moves you away from working "IN" your business to working "ON" your business? Remember: The tasks of the Technician and Doer may not be ignored or your business will certainly fail.

Take a few minutes and complete the chart below. Consider how you spent your time over the past month.

	What did you Do?	What did you Delegate?
As a TECHNICIAN…		
As a DOER…		
As a MANAGER…		
As a VISIONARY…		

Set Simple measurable steps that will lead you to accomplishing your goals.

	What will you Delegate?	What will you Do?
As a TECHNICIAN…		
As a DOER…		
As a MANAGER…		
As a VISIONARY…		

If you accomplish all of your goals over the next two/three/six months, <u>how will your position in your business look</u>? Remember: This tool is an informal inventory based on your perception of your business. The intended purpose of these exercises is to show you how to expand the possibilities within your business and to challenge your paradigms that currently define your business.

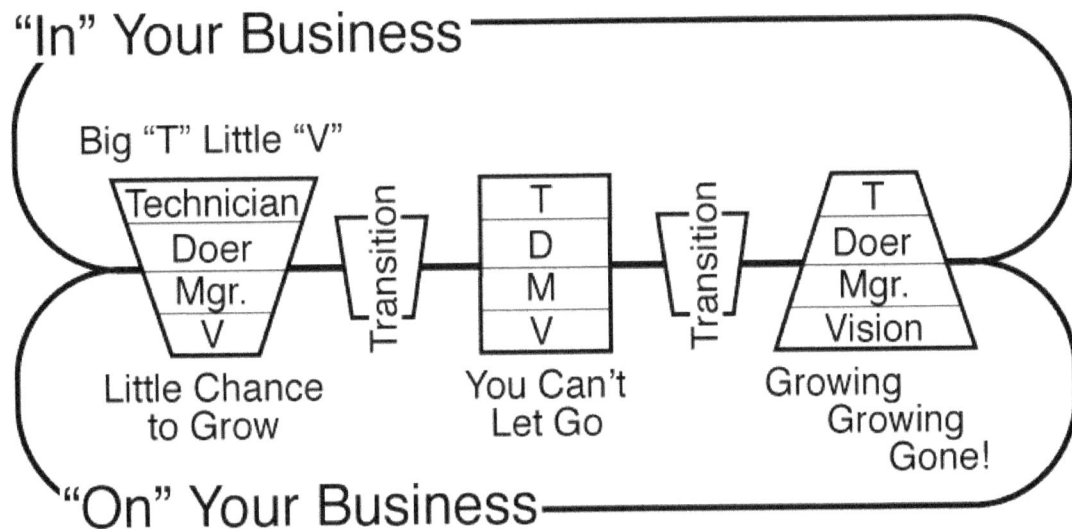

"In" Your Business

Big "T" Little "V"

Technician		T		T
Doer	Transition	D	Transition	Doer
Mgr.		M		Mgr.
V		V		Vision

| Little Chance to Grow | You Can't Let Go | Growing Growing Gone! |

"On" Your Business

In the end, if your days and weeks are dominated by the duties of the Technician and Doer, there is little hope for immediately growing your business. Some of us find it difficult to delegate and become overwhelmed with daily duties and the micro-managing of every task; you just "can't let go." In the mid-ground position, it is also impossible to grow your business, although you are a step closer to successful growth. This is a natural position for agents who are ready to grow because they have some experience and knowledge of the roles of manager and visionary. Remember: Transition times are important. It is no different than adjusting to closing fifty or one hundred units for the first time in a given year. Transition periods are uncomfortable and require perseverance. Remember, if you are feeling stuck or growing pains, this is the first section you may want to review.

The final section of this planning guide will be to take everything and put it into a Master Project List that will break down all of your goals to specific next steps.

SECTION D: How do I get there from here?
Part 17 - Creating a Master Project List

Step One: To achieve your "goals", you need to change them into "projects" which you will be actively working on over the next twelve months. From this, we will create a "Master Project List".

Review all of the goals you have created in all previous sections of this planning guide and list them here. Use more paper if necessary.

1. _____

2. _____

3. _____

4. _____

5. _____

6. _____

7. _____

8. _____

9. _____

10. _____

11. _____

12. _____

13. _____

14. _____

15. _____

16. _____

17. _____

18. _____

19. _____

20. _____

21. _____

22. _____

23. _____

24. _____

Master Project List: Step 2: Assigning Goals to Quarters

Assign each of the goals/projects listed above to a quarter next year.

First Quarter

1._____

2._____

3._____

4._____

5._____

6._____

Second Quarter

1._____

2._____

3._____

4._____

5._____

6._____

Third Quarter

1. _____

2. _____

3. _____

4. _____

5. _____

6. _____

Fourth Quarter

1. _____

2. _____

3. _____

4. _____

5. _____

6. _____

Master Project List: Step 3: Assigning Action Steps to Each Goal/Project
List the first one to two specific action steps needed to complete each project/goal.

Quarter 1:

1. (Goal)_____

  - (Action Step 1) _____

  - (Action Step 2) _____

2. _____

  - _____

  - _____

3. _____

  - _____

  - _____

4. _____

  - _____

  - _____

5. _____

  - _____

  - _____

6. _____

  - _____

  - _____

Quarter 2:

1. _____

  - _____
  - _____

2. _____

  - _____
  - _____

3. _____

  - _____
  - _____

4. _____

  - _____
  - _____

5. _____

  - _____
  - _____

6. _____

  - _____
  - _____

Quarter 3:

1. _____

   - _____

   - _____

2. _____

   - _____

   - _____

3. _____

   - _____

   - _____

4. _____

   - _____

   - _____

5. _____

   - _____

   - _____

6. _____

   - _____

   - _____

Quarter 4:

1. _____

- _____
- _____

2. _____

- _____
- _____

3. _____

- _____
- _____

4. _____

- _____
- _____

5. _____

- _____
- _____

6. _____

- _____
- _____

Conclusion:

The Master Project List must be reviewed weekly with each action step scheduled into your calendar. Each week you will have new "next steps" that will need to be scheduled as well. As a result, your Master Project List will be a living document that will change, grow and evolve weekly.

Congratulations!

You've taken time to complete this Life and Business Goal Setting and Business Planning Guide showing that you are serious about doing the work necessary to have the life you want to lead.

Now that you have completed this Planning Guide, contact my office to set you up your free coaching session to review your plan. All you need to do is contact me through my website at www.CheriAlguire.com and mention you would like to schedule your free Business Planning Workbook Review.

Just completing this process does not complete your journey. You will need to constantly review and analyze your numbers, break down your next steps, schedule them and then do the things you know you need to do. This will be an ongoing process you will review and add to throughout the year as you hone in on completing each task on the road to achieving your goals.

The most important thing that you can do to reach these important life goals is to have an accountability partner or coach to help keep you focused and on-track so that "everyday life" doesn't creep up on you and rob you of this focus. Your old ways can distract you from the steps you need to take to propel you forward.

Big goals, when looked at in their entirety, can tend to be overwhelming. When whittled down into smaller, easy-to-digest steps, you will find yourself able to, bit by bit, finish up each project. By being consistent with following this plan, I have no doubt you will hit your goals, achieve your dreams and create an amazing year and life for yourself.

Make it a GREAT Year!

~Coach Cheri

Free Business Planning Workbook Review Session

As a reward for finishing what you start, I will give you a free one-on-one coaching call with me (a $297 value) once you finish this workbook. All you need to do is contact me through my website at_CheriAlguire.com and mention you would like to schedule your free Business Planning Workbook Review Session.

For more resources, visit:

CheriAlguire.com
RealEstateBusinessPlanningGuide.com
ProBusinessAndLifeCoach.com
CoachCheri.com

If you have any questions about this or any other products or materials by Coach Cheri Alguire, please contact us at:

NLS Consulting, LLC
170 Rainbow Drive #7097
Livingston, TX 77399
(949) 916-3289
Info@CheriAlguire.com

www.ingramcontent.com/pod-product-compliance
Lightning Source LLC
Chambersburg PA
CBHW051229200326
41519CB00025B/7302